DEFENDING DOMESTIC BATTERY

Legal Strategies for Avoiding a Domestic Battery Conviction in Illinois

Jonathan E James Esq.

Copyright © 2019 by Jonathan James

All rights reserved. No part of this book may be used or reproduced in any manner whatsoever without written permission of the author

ISBN-13: 978-1-79-523793-2

CONTENTS

1	INTRODUCTION	1
2	WHAT IS DOMESTIC BATTERY IN ILLINOIS	6
3	THE PROCESS OF A DOMESTIC BATTERY CASE	10
4	WHAT ARE THE PENALTIES FOR DOMESTIC BATTERY?	22
5	ORDER OF PROTECTION	30
6	DOMESTIC BATTERY DEFENSES	42
	Can the alleged victim drop the charges?	44
	Can the alleged victim simply change their story?	45
	Spousal Privilege - Can my spouse be forced to testify against me?	48
	The Confrontation Clause - What If The Alleged Victim Does Not Show Up For Trial?	49
	Witness Credibility	50
	Medical Evidence	53
	Motions in Limine – Setting the Ground Rules for Trial	54
	Self Defense – What if I Was Attacked?	56
	Can My Prior History Be Used Against Me at Trial?	58
	What If The Police Never Read Me My Rights, Will My Case Be Dismissed?	60

7	POSSIBLE COMPANION CHARGES	64
8	POSSIBLE WAYS TO RESOLVE A DOMESTIC BATTERY CASE	70
	GLOSSARY	80
	ABOUT ATTORNEY JONATHAN JAMES	94

LEGAL DISCLAIMER

This book is for general information purposes only. This book gives a general overview of criminal domestic battery prosecutions in Illinois. This book is not legal advice and is not intended to provide specific legal advice or instruction on any specific situation. Reading this book does not create an attorney-client relationship between you and attorney Jonathan James, or the Law Office of Jonathan James, LLC. This book is based entirely on Illinois law. You should always direct any specific questions you have about your case to your own lawyer. No lawyer (including the author of this book) can ever make you any promises or guarantees about how your case will turn out.

CHAPTER 1

INTRODUCTION

I'm glad you decided to purchase a copy of this book on domestic battery in Illinois. This book can help you understand the options you have when facing domestic battery charges and what you should do to protect your rights. This book can help you answer many of the common questions you may have about a domestic battery charge such as:

- How serious is a domestic battery charge and what are the possible penalties?
- What is an order of protection?
- What is the "No Drop" policy?
- What if the alleged victim wants to drop the charges?
- What if the police didn't read me my rights?
- How long will this affect my record?
- What will happen to my firearm rights if I'm convicted?
- How do I fight a domestic battery charge?
- Do I need to hire a lawyer?

After reading this book you will be in a better position to decide if you need professional representation for your case.

As a Criminal Defense attorney in Illinois I have represented hundreds of people who have faced domestic battery charges. Most people who are forced to navigate our complex system of criminal justice are scared, confused and unsure about how to proceed with their case. This book is meant to be an introduction to the domestic battery laws in Illinois and what defense strategies can be used to help ensure the best possible outcome for your case.

Domestic battery cases are taken very seriously in Illinois and the legislature continues to stack the deck against individuals who are charged with domestic battery. For instance, domestic battery cases are not eligible for court supervision or any other disposition that may lead to a dismissal of the charges pending satisfactory completion of the sentence. The legislature also allows the prosecution to admit prior acts of domestic violence at trial, regardless of whether those acts were charged or led to a conviction. This is contrary to how other criminal cases within our court system are tried. For instance, if a person is charged with DUI, the prosecution will not be allowed to introduce evidence of any prior DUI convictions or charges the defendant may have.

Additionally, most jurisdictions in Illinois have adopted a "No Drop" policy when it comes to domestic battery cases. This means that the State will continue to prosecute the case even if the complaining witness recants their statements or wants to drop the charges. The State has also devoted extra funding and resources to the prosecution of domestic battery cases which includes assigning a victim advocate to every case, providing specialized training for domestic battery prosecutors, and assigning additional personnel to the domestic battery Unit in the State's Attorney's Office. This can be overwhelming for people who are facing domestic battery charges and can lead them to believe that their case is hopeless and that they should just plead guilty on the first court date to get it over. This is often a mistake as there are several collateral consequences to pleading guilty to a domestic battery charge including a lifetime ban on firearm ownership. Additionally, there are currently no mechanisms available to remove a domestic battery conviction from your record. If you are convicted of domestic battery that conviction will follow you the rest of your life. There is help available in every case, regardless of prior record or circumstances of the arrest. No case is ever hopeless.

Your first step should be to read this book in its entirety. Next, you should request a confidential case assessment with an experienced domestic battery defense attorney in your area. Most law offices, including mine, will offer you a free initial consultation to discuss your case and what steps you should take to protect your rights. If you are in the Northern Illinois area you may call my office to schedule your free initial case evaluation at 779-500-0167. We have offices located in Rockford, IL and Dekalb, IL.

EVERYONE WHO IS CHARGED WITH DOMESTIC BATTERY SHOULD MEET WITH A LAWYER BEFORE GOING TO COURT.

No lawyer can ever make you any promises or guarantees regarding the final result in a criminal case. Although this book discusses defense strategies that have assisted clients in the past achieve dismissals, not-guilty verdicts, or reductions to lesser charges, you should know that results obtained on behalf of one client do not necessarily indicate similar results can be obtained for other clients.

DEFENDING DOMESTIC BATTERY

CHAPTER 2

WHAT IS DOMESTIC BATTERY IN ILLINOIS?

The domestic battery laws in Illinois are constantly changing and the Legislature is always adding new penalties for persons convicted of domestic battery. Simply being charged with domestic battery can have a severe impact on your job, educational opportunities, and your right to own a firearm. The laws concerning domestic battery are very complicated and if you are facing domestic battery charges, it is important that you act quickly in order to protect your rights.

Most people believe that to be convicted of domestic battery, the offender must be married to the alleged victim and inflict some sort of injury. The domestic battery laws in Illinois have been adapted to encompass a wide range of behaviors and relationships between the offender and the alleged victim. In fact, no injury is even necessary for the State to get a conviction for domestic battery. The law provides that the offender only needs to *"make physical contact of an insulting or provoking* nature with a family or household member." The phrase *"insulting or provoking nature"* is often left to the jury figure out and there is no bright line rule. I have seen the State prosecute domestic battery cases involving contact that did not seem to meet the requirement of *"insulting and provoking nature"* including: a husband slapping his wife's hand when she attempted to take her husband's property, a husband tossing a remote to his wife across the room and the wife did not catch the remote and instead hit her incidentally, a boyfriend trying to retrieve his cellphone after his girlfriend took it and threatened to break it, and the list goes on.

Additionally, there is no requirement that an offender be married to the alleged victim in order to be charged with domestic battery. The law only requires that the defendant be a *"family or household member"* of the alleged victim and include all of the following relationships:

- Boyfriend/Girlfriend
- Ex-wife/Ex-husband
- Ex-girlfriend/Ex-boyfriend
- Parents/Children
- Parents/Step-Children
- A couple that shares a child but is not in a relationship
- Persons who share or formerly shared a common dwelling
- Siblings
- and many more

The only difference between the charge of *"domestic battery"* and *"battery"* is that the alleged victim falls into one of these enumerated categories. While the distinction is slight, the potential impact on the person charged is significant. In Illinois, a domestic battery charge is not eligible for any special disposition, like court supervision, which can lead to a dismissal of the charges at the end of the supervision period, and if you are convicted of domestic battery there is no way to have the charge sealed or expunged from your record. Additionally, any person who is accused of domestic battery will not be allowed to possess any firearms during the pendency of the case, even if they are eventually acquitted of the charges. In order to regain the right to own a firearm after being charged with domestic battery, the charge must be dismissed, reduced, or the case taken to trial and adjudicated not guilty. After the case is resolved in one of these manners, the defendant will have to reapply for a FOID card.

What rights do I have when talking to the Police?

Prior to making an arrest, the police may question you. This will either happen at the scene shortly after an alleged incident, or if the incident is reported after the fact, the police may try to call you and ask questions about the incident. It is important to know that any statements you make to the police, or anyone else, are admissible in court and can be used as evidence against you. The police will try to ask you questions and get you to make statements against your interest. You are never required to make any statements to the police and you have a right to have an attorney present during any questioning. If you wish to exercise your constitutional rights, you must be assertive and clear when dealing with law enforcement. You must indicate to the officer that you will not answer any questions without legal counsel present. If the officer tries to continue the interrogation, and many of them do, you must repeat your request to remain silent and not answer any questions without an attorney present.

CHAPTER 3

THE PROCESS OF A DOMESTIC BATTERY CASE

Domestic battery cases often begin when the police are called to investigate an incident. These calls often come within close proximity to an alleged incident but can occur much later. Usually these calls are initiated by the alleged victim, but can come from friends or family who were nearby during an argument, or random bystanders who witnessed a couple arguing. While the information contained in these calls is often exaggerated or an outright fabrication, the Illinois rules of evidence will, in most circumstances, allow the admission of these 911 calls at trial even though they are technically hearsay. This is done through the *excited utterance* exception to the hearsay rule. If the prosecutor lays the proper foundation, these calls may be admitted into evidence even if the caller is not available to testify at trial.

Collecting Evidence and Witness Statements

Once a police department receives a call for assistance, police officers will be dispatched to the scene. Usually there will be more than one officer dispatched to a domestic battery complaint. This enables the officers to separate the parties involved and get everyone's side of the story. While police officers are trained to get both sides of the story, there have been cases where officers will only talk to the complaining witness and make an arrest without speaking to the other party. When police only get one side of the story, it is often the case that the complaining party has exaggerated or fabricated events in order to get the other party arrested.

In addition to witness statements, the police will also photograph injuries that might have occurred to either party, photograph the scene for damaged property or other indicia of a struggle, and collect any pieces of evidence that they may deem relevant. After the police have collected statements from all the witnesses on scene and processed the evidence, they will regroup and talk amongst themselves to determine what action should be taken. Police are trained to make an arrest if they believe a domestic battery might have occurred. This belief may be based on incomplete information or fabricated statements. Once they have determined a domestic battery has occurred, someone is going to jail. The complaining witness may say "*I don't want to press charges*", or "*I'm not signing a written complaint*", but none of this factors into the officer's decision to make an arrest.

Arrest and Bond

Once someone is arrested for domestic battery, they will be taken to jail for processing. This involves taking a mug shot, finger prints and being housed at the jail until that person can be brought in front of a judge to get their bond set. While most misdemeanor cases in Illinois can have bond set by the police officer, domestic battery cases are the exception and the arrested party will have to wait in custody until the next day (or possibly the day after next depending on the court schedule) to have bond set by a judge.

When the accused is finally brought before the judge, bond will be set and the accused will need to post a certain amount of money to secure their release. In addition to the money posted, the accused will also have to comply with any additional conditions the judge may place on their release. Usual bond conditions may include: No contact with the alleged victim, no consumption of drugs or alcohol, random urinalysis testing, and stay away from the residence of the alleged victim. Different judges will place different conditions upon people charged with domestic battery.

If the accused and the alleged victim share a residence, and there is a no-contact bond condition, the accused will be barred from returning home and will likely need to find a new place to stay during the pendency of the case, or until a judge signs an order modifying the bond condition. If the accused wishes to remove property from the shared residence, they will have to contact the Sheriff's Department to make arrangement to pick up their belongings. This is usually done under the supervision of a Sheriff's Deputy and then, once their items are removed, they will have to get special permission from the court to return to the residence or to have contact with the alleged victim.

Modifying Bond Conditions

It is possible, and sometimes necessary, to modify the original bond conditions set by the court. To do this, the defendant will have to file a motion to modify conditions of bond and specify which bond condition they seek to modify and why the modification is necessary. Many times, a no contact provision may be detrimental to the alleged victim. For instance, if the alleged victim and the defendant are married, living in the same home, or raising children together, then the no contact bond condition may need to be modified in order to keep the family unit functional.

Once a motion to modify bond is filed, it will be set for a hearing. During the hearing, evidence will be presented to the court and the judge will determine whether to grant the defendant's request. If the defendant is asking for contact with the alleged victim, it will be necessary to have the alleged victim testify in open court in support of the defendant's request. The alleged victim will not necessarily address the allegations contained within the charging document, but they will need to affirm on the record that they want to have contact with the defendant. Additionally, the alleged victim will need to testify that they are not afraid of the defendant, and if any other incident arose in the future, they would not hesitate to contact the police.

Even with supporting testimony from the alleged victim, the court may not grant the defendant's request for contact. When deciding on a request to modify bond conditions, the court will consider: the defendant's criminal history, the allegations in the charging document, a brief proffer by the State's Attorney on the allegations against the defendant, and any testimony taken at hearing. The court could grant the request outright, grant the request conditioned on the defendant enrolling in treatment or performing other tasks, partially grant the request by limiting the time or method of contact the defendant may have with the alleged victim, or deny the request.

Charging Decisions – Prosecutorial Discretion

Throughout the whole process of a domestic battery case, the biggest wild card is going to be the prosecutor's discretion. The laws in Illinois strongly favor the prosecution and conviction of individuals who are accused of domestic battery. The severity of the charge against the accused as well as what type of disposition is offered is placed squarely on the shoulders of the prosecutor. While there are some mechanisms in place that allow a defendant to challenge a prosecutor's charging decision, these are usually not very effective. If someone wants to challenge a domestic battery case in the face of a prosecuting entity that only wants to see everyone convicted and receive the harshest possible punishment, they will likely have to set their case for a jury trial, often on an inflated charge.

When making their charging decision the prosecutor is going to look at the alleged facts of the case, as contained in a police report, and the accused's prior criminal history. Then the prosecutor will charge the case under one of several statutes that are applicable to domestic battery. Domestic battery is considered a class A misdemeanor which is punishable by up to a year in jail, probation up to 2 years and fines and cost of up to $2,500. A domestic battery charge may be enhanced to a felony based on prior record or the circumstances of the case.

Once a charging decision is made, the prosecutor will have to create a complaint for misdemeanor cases or they will have to seek a bill of indictment for felony cases. Should the prosecutor elect to charge the case as a felony, they will have to get a bill of indictment by presenting their case to a grand jury or setting the case for a preliminary hearing.

Grand Jury / Preliminary Hearing

Grand Juries or preliminary hearings are only applicable to felony cases. Prior to a defendant officially being charged with a felony case in Illinois, there needs to be a probable cause determination. The Illinois justice system allows prosecutors to accomplish this in one of 2 ways, by presenting their evidence to a grand jury or by having a preliminary hearing in front of a judge. Prosecutors prefer the Grand Jury method, because it is easier to get a bill of indictment as opposed to having a preliminary hearing. However, some counties prefer the preliminary hearing process because it is cheaper, in that they do not have to pay for jurors and transcripts for every single felony case they wish to charge. These processes differ in who makes the probable cause determination and who gets to ask witnesses questions.

A Grand Jury is a secretive process that neither the defendant, nor the defendant's attorney may attend. During a Grand Jury hearing, the prosecutor will call one or more prosecution friendly witnesses to testify before the grand jury, which is made up of 12 members from the community. Unlike a trial by jury that requires all jurors to agree on a verdict, a Grand Jury only needs 9 members of the jury to agree that the state has met its burden. The witnesses that are called to testify are usually police officers or somehow related to law enforcement and the prosecutor will ask them a series of leading questions that address the elements of the offense charged. The State may also present exhibits and other evidence, but this is usually not necessary. Since the State will be conducting several Grand Juries in a day, they will quickly read through the officer's police report asking questions that only require the police officer to answer in the affirmative. At the end of the presentation of witnesses and evidence, the Court will then ask the Grand Jury to decide if the State has presented enough evidence to establish probable cause for the case that is charged. Probable cause is a very low bar for the State to hurdle and is significantly lower than the burden they have at trial which is proof beyond a reasonable doubt. Additionally, the rules of evidence really don't apply at a grand jury proceeding and the prosecutor will be allowed to lead their witness, elicit hearsay testimony, and allow speculation from unqualified witnesses. Even if the rules of evidence were followed at these proceedings, there is no defense counsel present to object.

A preliminary hearing is different from a Grand Jury in that it is a judge, not a jury, that makes the determination as to whether the State has met its burden of proof. Like a Grand Jury, a Preliminary Hearing is also subject to relaxed rules of evidence and the court will allow hearsay and other testimony that is not admissible in a trial setting. Also, in a preliminary hearing, the defendant and the defendant's counsel may be present and defense counsel may cross examine any witnesses that the State presents. Additionally, after the State rests its case, the defendant may present witnesses and evidence on his own behalf. This, however, is rare because the defendant is not provided with any discovery materials prior to the hearing, such as, police reports, witness statements, videos, etc. that the state will be using to prosecute the case. Essentially, the defendant is going into the hearing blind. If the defendant were to take the stand, he would be subject to cross-examination by the State and any statements that he made would be admissible at trial and any subsequent hearings. Most defense attorneys prefer to keep their client off the stand and not give the State a free shot at cross-examination before trial. Once the defense rests their case, the judge will then make a ruling as to whether the state has met its very low burden of probable cause.

Regardless of whether the State uses a grand jury or a preliminary hearing, their burden of proof is low, and these usually equate to nothing more than a rubber stamp process. However, in the rare circumstance that the State fails to meet its burden of proof at a preliminary hearing, they may elect to then take their case to a grand jury in order to get a probable cause determination. Likewise, if the grand jury returns no probable cause, the State may set their case for a preliminary hearing. Essentially, the State can get two bites at the apple if they do not succeed at their first probable cause hearing. Because of the low burden of proof and the relaxed rules of evidence it is rare that a felony case will get dismissed based on a probable cause hearing.

Arraignment

Whether the domestic battery case is charged as a felony or a misdemeanor, the first court date is usually to allow the defendant to be arraigned. An arraignment is part of the criminal procedure that occurs in a courtroom before a judge. The purpose of an arraignment is to let the defendant know what he is being charged with and to provide the defendant with a copy of the charging document. For misdemeanor cases, the charging document is only an information that lays out the statute under which the defendant is being charged, the class of the charge, the possible penalties, and a very brief summation of facts that address the elements of the statute charged. For felony cases, the charging document is a Bill of Indictment that is tendered to the defendant in open court. The Bill of Indictment details all charges that the defendant is facing as well as the possible penalties. Like an information for misdemeanor cases, the Bill of Indictment will contain the relevant statutes and a brief summation of facts that addresses the elements of that crime that is charged. During the arraignment process the court will advise the defendant of his rights and ensure he understands the possible penalties associated with all of the charges. After these advisements, the defendant will enter a plea to all of the charges. If there is no deal that is worked out with the State, the defendant will enter a plea of not guilty and the case will be continued. If there is a disposition that is amenable to all parties, that may be presented to the court for its approval. However, having a disposition on the arraignment date is extremely rare.

Pretrial Conference / Status Hearings

After the arraignment and prior to trial, the court will likely set the case over for a status hearing, or what is commonly referred to as a pretrial conference. These are usually necessary to give the State an opportunity to provide the Defense with discovery materials in open court, such as police reports, witness statements, 911 recordings, videos, medical documentation of any alleged injuries, etc. The pretrial conference also allows either side to file any motions that they feel are necessary prior to trial. If an agreement between the parties is reached, depending on the judge and the courtroom protocols, it may be possible to present the agreement to the court during the pretrial conference and resolve the case then and there. Sometimes, a judge will not take a plea on certain pretrial dates due to constraints on the court's time and will reset the case for plea on a special date when the court has more time.

Motion Hearings

Prior to trial it might be necessary to get the court to rule on a motion, which would essentially set the rules for what evidence each side may present at trial. Usual motions that the Defense may file would include a motion to suppress evidence, a motion to suppress statements, a motion to introduce the violent tendencies of the alleged victim when the Defense is claiming self-defense, or a motion-in-limine to restrict what the state may present at a trial, such as excluding potential hearsay evidence.

The State will often present motions that allow for the admission of evidence that is usually not admissible in other types of cases. These are usually motions-in-limine where the State will ask the court to allow the introduction of evidence such as any prior incidences of domestic violence alleged to have been committed by the defendant. The bar for admission of this type of evidence is very low and include prior acts that may not have been charged or even reported to the police. Even though the defendant has a presumption of innocence for these uncharged prior acts of alleged domestic violence, the Illinois Legislature says that these acts are relevant and admissible at trial and only require the State to show minimal foundation for their admission. Additionally, the prosecution may also try to introduce statements the alleged victim made while calling 911 or statements given to the police. While these statements are technically hearsay, the court may allow them under the excited utterance exception to the hearsay rule. The prosecution may do this when they have an alleged victim that is not cooperative with the prosecution and may not show up for the trial. While proceeding forward with a prosecution where the defendant's accuser is not available for cross examination seems like a pretty egregious violation of a the defendant's 6th amendment rights, Illinois courts have upheld convictions where the alleged victim in domestic battery cases has not been available for trial.

Plea

The prosecutor will usually, but not always, make an offer to resolve the case without it going to trial. The offer tendered by the state is subject to negotiation. If acceptable terms can be reached, then the case can be resolved with a plea. A plea bargain may include an amended charge, a reduced charge, or an offer of deferred prosecution, assuming such a program is available in the county prosecuting the case. Most counties do not offer deferred prosecution for domestic battery cases. Plea negotiations are an ongoing process and offers will vary over time based on the prosecutor's communication with the alleged victim, communications with other parties involved in the case, and mitigating factors that are applicable to the defendant.

Once a plea agreement has been reached, it still needs to be accepted by the court. This is done in open court. The parties recite the terms of the agreement and the court can either accept or reject the terms. If the court rejects the terms, then the parties can either renegotiate the agreement or the case may be set for trial.

Trial

If the parties are unable to reach an agreement, then the case will proceed to trial. There are two types of trials that are available for domestic battery cases. A jury trial, where evidence will be presented to 12 members of the community and they will decide the question of guilt or innocence, or a bench trial, where a judge will determine the question of guilt or innocence. The type of trial is determined exclusively by the defendant. The State, the judge, and even the defendant's attorney cannot force a defendant to accept one type of trial over the other.

CHAPTER 4

WHAT ARE THE PENALTIES FOR DOMESTIC BATTERY?

Every domestic battery conviction, regardless of prior record or circumstances of the offense, will involve a lifetime revocation of firearm ownership and a permanent criminal record that cannot be sealed or expunged. Additionally, a domestic battery charge can have severe criminal penalties that can involve jail time or even time in the Department of Corrections depending on the severity of the charge and the defendant's prior record. In addition to all the criminal penalties for domestic battery, there are several collateral consequences that may be associated with a conviction, even for first time offenders. These may include:

- Difficulty finding a job or obtaining professional license
- Disqualification from admission to colleges, or possible expulsion if already enrolled in college
- Lifetime ban on firearm ownership
- Removal or exclusions from entry to the United States for non-citizens

- Restrictions on where you can live
- Potentially harmful to any pending child custody matter.

Misdemeanor Domestic Battery

For a first time domestic battery charge, this will usually be charged as a class A misdemeanor which has a range of penalties including up to one year in jail and fines of up to $2,500 (plus additional mandatory fees). Special dispositions like Chapter 20 probation and court supervision are NOT available in domestic battery cases and any plea will result in a criminal conviction.

Possible Penalties for Misdemeanor Domestic Battery

- Up to one year in jail
- Fine up to $2,500
- Probation or Conditional Discharge up to two years
- Lifetime revocation of firearm ownership
- Permanent criminal record that cannot be sealed or expunged
- If there is an injury proven as part of the case, then the defendant would not receive day-for-day credit on jail time.

Felony Domestic Battery

In Illinois, there are several ways that a domestic battery can become a felony. Even if it is your first offense for domestic battery, your case can still be enhanced to a felony under certain circumstances. The approach to representing a client charged with a felony domestic battery is drastically different than representing a client with a misdemeanor domestic battery charge. It is imperative that a fully comprehensive defense strategy be designed and implemented as soon as possible after an arrest in order to provide for the best possible outcome.

Class 4 Felony Domestic Battery

A domestic battery case can be enhanced to a class 4 felony based on prior record. The State has the option of charging a domestic battery as a class 4 felony if the defendant has one or two prior convictions for any of the following charges:

- Domestic Battery
- Aggravated Domestic Battery
- Aggravated Battery
- Heinous Battery
- Stalking
- Criminal Sexual Assault
- Kidnapping
- Unlawful Restraint
- Aggravated Arson
- First Degree Murder
- Violation of an Order of Protection

While the elements for a misdemeanor domestic battery and a class 4 felony domestic battery enhanced based on prior record are the same, the possible penalties are drastically different. With a class 4 felony domestic battery, the possible penalties may include a stay in the Department of Corrections between 1 and 3 years in addition to a fine of up to $25,000.

Possible Penalties for Class 4 Domestic Battery

- Possible imprisonment in the Department of Corrections between 1 and 3 years.
- If the felony is extended term eligible, possible imprisonment between 1 and 6 years
- Probation or Conditional Discharge up to 30 months in length
- Periodic Imprisonment up to 18 months in length
- Minimum 3 days in jail in addition to any other penalties that may be imposed
- If committed in the presence of a child less than 18 years old, then an additional
    - 10 days in jail or 300 hours of public service work or both
    - Pay for the cost of counselling that the child may require
- Permanent felony conviction
- Fine of up to $25,000

Class 3 felony Domestic Battery

A domestic battery case can be enhanced to a class 3 felony based on prior record. The State has the option of charging a domestic battery as a class 3 felony if the defendant has three prior convictions for domestic battery.

Possible Penalties for Class 3 Domestic Battery

- Possible imprisonment in the Department of Corrections between 2 and 5 years.
- If the felony is extended term eligible, possible imprisonment between 2 and 10 years
- Probation or Conditional Discharge up to 30 months in length
- Periodic Imprisonment up to 18 months in length
- Minimum 3 days in jail in addition to any other penalties that may be imposed
- If committed in the presence of a child less than 18 years old then an additional
    - 10 days in jail or 300 hours of public service work or both
    - Pay for the cost of counselling that the child may require
- Permanent felony conviction

Class 2 Felony Domestic Battery

Domestic battery is a Class 2 felony if the defendant has 4 or more prior convictions for domestic battery under the laws of Illinois, or 4 or more prior convictions under the law of another jurisdiction for any offense which is substantially similar.

Possible Penalties for Class 2 Domestic Battery

- Possible imprisonment in the Department of Corrections between 3 and 7 years.
- If the felony is extended term eligible, possible imprisonment between 3 and 14 years
- Probation or Conditional Discharge up to 48 months in length
- Periodic Imprisonment from 18 to 30 months
- Minimum 3 days in jail in addition to any other penalties that may be imposed
- If committed in the presence of a child less than 18 years old then an additional
    - 10 days in jail or 300 hours of public service work or both
    - Pay for the cost of counselling that the child may require
- Permanent felony conviction

Aggravated Domestic Battery – Class 2 Felony

Aggravated Domestic Battery is a Class 2 Felony and does not depend on prior record. The State has the option to charge Aggravated Domestic Battery against any person who, in committing a domestic battery, does one of the following

- Knowingly causes great bodily harm, or permanent disability or disfigurement.
- Strangles another individual.

The phrase "strangle" means intentionally impeding the normal breathing or circulation of the blood of an individual by applying pressure on the throat or neck of that individual or by blocking the nose or mouth of that individual.

Possible Penalties for Aggravated Domestic Battery

- Possible imprisonment in the Department of Corrections between 3 and 7 years.
- If the felony is extended term eligible, possible imprisonment between 3 and 14 years
- Probation or Conditional Discharge up to 48 months in length
- Periodic Imprisonment from 18 to 30 months
- If the defendant receives a sentence of Probation or Conditional discharge, they must serve a minimum of 60 days in jail.
- Minimum 3 days in jail in addition to any other penalties that may be imposed if this is a second or subsequent offense for Domestic Battery or Aggravated Domestic Battery.
- If committed in the presence of a child less than 18 years old then an additional
  - 10 days in jail or 300 hours of public service work or both
  - Pay for the cost of counselling that the child may require
- Permanent felony conviction

CHAPTER 5

ORDER OF PROTECTION

In addition to bond conditions that are set on persons charged with domestic battery, it is possible for the alleged victim in the case to seek an order of protection. Orders of protection are court orders that are designed to protect one family or household member from the actions of another. They are governed by the Illinois Domestic Violence Act. An order of protection is a civil order and not criminal in nature. However, if the order of protection is granted and the Respondent violates the terms of the order, then the State may file criminal charges. These charges would be for violation of an order of protection and would be in addition to any domestic battery charge that the state has previously filed.

An order of protection is only issued after the person seeking the order of protection files a petition with the court and has their case heard in front of a judge. The usual remedy for an order of protection is to keep one party away from another. However, there are circumstances where an order of protection may require a Respondent to do a lot more than simply stay away from another person. The relief available in an order of protection may include the following:

- Stop harassing, abusing, stalking, and intimidating a protected party.
- Stop interfering with a protected party's personal liberty.
- Bar a Respondent from a shared residence.
- Require a Respondent to stay away from a shared home while under the influence of drugs or alcohol.
- Require a Respondent to attend counselling.
- Require a Respondent to stay away from a protected party's work, school or any other place specified by the order.
- Not have any contact with the protected party including, text messages, social media, and phone calls.
- Respondent must surrender their FOID card and surrender any firearms owned during the term of the order of protection.
- Prohibit the Respondent from taking a child out of state.
- Limit or restrict custody of children. Custody arrangements are subject to visitation as defined in the order of protection.
- Custody of any household pets.
- Require a Respondent to turn over certain personal property and may be ordered to refrain from damaging other personal property that is co-owned with the Petitioner.
- Require a Respondent to pay child support, child counselling, and any losses the Petitioner may have suffered as a result of the Respondent's actions.
- Any other condition that the Court considers reasonable for the protection of the Petitioner.

How a person gets an order of protection

To get an order of protection, a person must file a petition with the Circuit Court asking that an order be entered against a family or household member to limit or restrict certain types of contact and activities. Usually the Clerk of the Circuit Court will have a dedicated window exclusively for servicing orders of protections. This window is usually staffed with personnel specially trained in handling these types of cases. When filing a petition for an order of protection, the Petitioner must list all the reasons they are seeking an order of protection. Once the petition is filed, the Petitioner will in short order have a hearing in front of a judge. In this initial hearing, the Petitioner will be sworn in, the judge will read the petition and may ask additional questions of the Petitioner. This is usually a very brief hearing and the only evidence that is taken will be the word of the Petitioner as contained in the petition and as testified to in front of the judge. The offending party listed in the petition will not be present and they will not be able to challenge the credibility of the allegations in the petition. The judge will simply consider that if all the allegations are true, would an order of protection be warranted.

Courts will grant an order of protection if the Petitioner proves three elements:

1. That the Petitioner (or a protected party on whose behalf the petition has been filed) is a "family or household member" of the Respondent.
2. That the Respondent has "abused" the Petitioner (or a protected party); and
3. That the court has jurisdiction to hear the case.

The term abuse is defined within the Illinois Domestic Violence Act as *"physical abuse, harassment, intimidation of a dependent, interference with personal liberty or willful deprivation but does not include reasonable direction of a minor child by a parent or person in loco parentis."*

If the Petitioner has alleged the three elements above in their petition, the judge will grant an Emergency order of protection and then set the case out for a hearing on a plenary (or more permanent) order of protection. During the hearing for the plenary order of protection, the Respondent will be present and will be allowed to challenge the accusations set forth in the petition. The Respondent may cross examine any of the Petitioner's witnesses, call witnesses, and present evidence to contradict the Petitioner's allegations

Emergency Order of Protection

An emergency order of protection is also referred to as an ex-parte order of protection, because it is heard without the Respondent being present to challenge the sufficiency of the allegations contained in the petition. All a person needs to do to obtain an emergency order of protection is to allege, under oath, that a family or household member abused them within the jurisdiction. The credibility of the allegations will not be challenged at an emergency order of protection hearing and the only people present will be the judge and the Petitioner.

Once the emergency order of protection is granted by the judge, the next step will be to serve a copy of the order on the Respondent. An Emergency order of protection is not effective until it is served on the Respondent and this service is usually effectuated by the Sheriff's Department. Once the Respondent is given notice of the order, they are bound by all the conditions contained within the order. These conditions usually include: not having any contact with the Petitioner or protected party as listed by the Petitioner, stay away from the protected party's residence or place of work, and in certain circumstances, the court may even determine distribution of property, child support and child custody. Additionally, anyone who is subject to an order of protection will have to surrender their FOID card and will not be able to possess a firearm while the order of protection is active.

Plenary Order of Protection

A plenary order of protection is a more permanent order of protection and usually lasts 2 years but can be modified by agreement of the parties or order of the court. Before the court can issue a Plenary order of protection, the Respondent must be given an opportunity to respond to the allegations in the petition. Once the Respondent is served with the petition and the emergency order of protection, they will have an opportunity to prepare a defense to the allegations. Even though an order or protection is civil in nature, Illinois law says that the criminal rules of evidence will control the order of protection hearing. This is significant because it will prevent the Respondent from sending interrogatories and conducting depositions upon the Petitioner. However, the Respondent may still serve the Petitioner with a motion for discovery asking for any evidence that may be used at the hearing. This includes medical records that may have been related to the allegations in the petition, text messages or other communications referenced in the petition, photographs of injuries or damaged property, etc.

After the discovery process is completed and both sides have collected sufficient records and information from the other, the petition will be set for a hearing. At a hearing, both sides will be allowed to call witnesses and submit evidence to either challenge or support the allegation in the petition. There is a wide range of evidence that may be presented at an order of protection hearing including:

- Third party witnesses that were present during the allegations
- Text messages sent between the parties
- Medical records
- Photographs of any injuries or property damage
- Testimony from the parties usually offering their recollection of the alleged events.

There is no right to a jury trial during an order of protection hearing and a judge will be the trier of fact. Prior to having a hearing on the order of protection, the Respondent must file with the court, a meritorious defense to the allegations in the petition. At hearing, the judge will be charged with deciding whether the events alleged by the Petitioner are true, and if they are true, would those allegations warrant an order of protection. To have the order of protection granted, the Petitioner will have to prove, by a preponderance of the evidence, that the Petitioner is a household member that has been abused by the Respondent within the jurisdiction.

How an Order of Protection Can be Violated

Once a judge grants the Petitioner's order of protection, that order will contain several things the Respondent will be prevented from doing and in some cases, will include things that the

Respondent will be required to do. If a Respondent does any of the prohibited activities, the State may file criminal charges against the Respondent for violation of an order of protection. These prohibited activities usually include contact with the alleged victim or any other protected party, contact with a protected party's home address or place of employment, or using a third party to facilitate contact with a protected party.

If the parties in an order of protection are married or have children together, it is possible for the order of protection to address possession of assets, child support, and child visitation. For a married couple with children, an order of protection will serve as a mini-divorce and there will be a resolution for a lot of items that are usually settled in a divorce case. These orders for child support, visitation, and distribution of assets will last as long as the order of protection is effective or it is superseded by an order for a dissolution of marriage.

Penalties for Violating an Order of Protection

While an order of protection is civil in nature, violation of an order of protection can lead to criminal charges. When the Petitioner feels that an order of protection has been violated, they may contact the police and report the violating behavior. The police will then be able to look at the order issued by the judge and they will make a field determination whether they think the order has been violated. If the police feel the order has been violated, which can be a very low bar such as the Respondent sending a text message, then the police will either arrest the offending party if they are present, or they will seek an arrest warrant from a judge for the offending party.

A first offense violation of an order of protection is usually charged as a class A misdemeanor, which can involve up to a year in jail, a fine of up to $2,500 plus court costs, and probation or conditional discharge for up to 2 years.

A violation of an order of protection can be charged as a Class 4 felony based on the defendant's prior record. If a person commits a violation of an order of protection and has previously been convicted of any of the following:

- Domestic Battery
- Violation of an Order of Protection
- Murder/Attempted Murder
- Aggravated Battery
- Stalking
- Criminal Sexual Assault
- Kidnapping
- Unlawful Restraint
- Aggravated Arson
- Assault of a Child
- Aggravated Discharge of a Firearm

A Class 4 Felony Violation of an Order of Protection has a possible sentence of 1 to 3 years in the Department of Corrections.

The court shall impose a minimum penalty of 24 hours imprisonment for a defendant's second or subsequent violation of any order of protection; unless the court explicitly finds that an increased penalty or such period of imprisonment would be manifestly unjust.

Fighting an Order of Protection

A lot of people named as respondents in an order of protection case do not attempt to challenge the allegations. Many people believe if they do not want to have contact with a person then there is no harm in having the order of protection in place. This is often a mistake as there are several consequences to having an order of protection, even if the order is not violated. First, anyone with an active order of protection against them, whether it is an emergency order of protection or a plenary order of protection, will have their FOID card revoked and they will have to surrender any firearms in their possession. Additionally, there may be conditions in the order of protection that may require the Respondent to stay away from certain locations in addition to the Petitioner's place of residence, such as their children's school or a place of worship. Finally, there may be conditions in an order of protection that may require the Respondent to do certain things, such as pay child support, turn over certain property, or enroll in treatment.

Fighting an order of protection is not a simple task and if you are named as the Respondent, it will be an uphill battle. The legislature has crafted the laws such that they are *"liberally construed"* to favor the Petitioner. Unlike other civil proceedings, the Respondent will not be allowed to submit interrogatories to the Petitioner or depose witnesses. Additionally, recent changes in the law now require the Respondent to file a meritorious defense that is verified and supported by affidavit. The verified notice and affidavit shall set forth the evidence that will be presented at a hearing. If this is not done, the Respondent will waive their right to hearing.

Even if a Respondent does not wish to have contact with the

Petitioner, they should still attempt to challenge the order of protection. Even though orders of protection are civil in nature, there is a mix of civil and criminal rules that control the proceeding. The rules of criminal procedure will control discovery, venue, and penalties for untrue statements. The rules of civil procedure will be used for all other aspects of the process. Because the criminal rules of discovery are observed for orders of protection, the Respondent will be barred from sending interrogatories or conducting depositions, but they may file a motion for discovery and require the Petitioner to produce documents and other evidence that may be used at hearing.

Often, a Petitioner will fabricate allegations when seeking an order of protection, because they think it will gain them an advantage in a divorce or custody case. These false allegations should be challenged by using discovery requests. Discovery requests will require the Petitioner to produce the evidence that may be relevant to the allegations in the petition. If the Petitioner is claiming an injury, then medical records should be requested. If there are allegations of damaged property, then photos of the damage and repair estimates should be turned over. A Respondent should never go into an order of protection hearing without having every piece of evidence the Petitioner may attempt to use. By filing timely discovery requests and serving it on the Petitioner, the Respondent can guarantee that they will not be surprised at hearing. If the Petitioner tries to use evidence that was requested by the Respondent and not turned over, then it will be barred by the court.

Once the discovery requests are made and the evidence is collected, the Respondent should start to prepare their case. This will involve cross-examining the Petitioner and finding witnesses to support their version of events. The Respondent should find as many witnesses as possible to contradict the Petitioner's version of events.

At an order of protection hearing, the Petitioner will have the burden of proof. That means, if the Petitioner does not present any evidence to the court, their petition will be dismissed. Because an order of protection is civil in nature, the burden of proof will be preponderance of the evidence, or more likely than not to have occurred. This is different than criminal trials, where the burden of proof is beyond a reasonable doubt. However, recent changes in the law now require a Respondent to file a meritorious defense prior to challenging an order of protection.

Since the Petitioner must prove their case, they will go first at hearing. This usually involves them being sworn in and giving testimony about the incidents alleged in their petition. If the Petitioner tries to talk about anything not alleged in the petition, the Respondent should object based on relevance and being outside the scope of the hearing. Also, if the Petitioner tries to talk about something someone else said, then the Respondent should object on the basis of hearsay. When cross-examining the Petitioner, the Respondent should go into great detail about the circumstances surrounding the event. Ask why the Petitioner did or did not do certain things that a normal person would have done, had their allegations been true. For instance, if the Petitioner is claiming an injury but did not call the police or go to the hospital. Most people will call the police when they are attacked and seek treatment for injuries. If they did not do this, it is likely because the story is a fabrication.

A quality cross-examination will be the best defense to an order of protection. This should be thoroughly prepared ahead of time using the allegations in the petition and the materials received through the discovery process. The cross-examiner will have to think on their feet and adapt to the flow of the hearing. Attention to detail is key, and extensive notes should be taken during the hearing. A partial closing argument should be prepared ahead of time, and it should be supplemented by the testimony that is given during the hearing. I like printing out my argument with space available for me to write in additional comments as the hearing progresses.

CHAPTER 6

DOMESTIC BATTERY DEFENSES

Defending a domestic battery case can be more complicated than defending other criminal cases because the legislature continues to make special laws that stack the deck in favor of the prosecution. For instance, during a domestic battery trial, the State may admit into evidence any prior act of domestic violence alleged to have been committed by the defendant. The defendant does not have to be convicted or even charged with these acts for them to be admissible. The prosecution may call any witness they see fit, put them on the stand and they may testify about any prior instance of domestic violence that may have occurred, whether there was a finding of guilt or whether the case was even reported to the police. This is in stark contrast to how other cases are prosecuted. For instance, in prosecutions for DUI or retail theft, the prosecutor will not be allowed to introduce into evidence any prior act for DUI or theft, even if the defendant was found guilty of those prior charges.

Moreover, the majority of prosecuting agencies in Illinois have implemented a "No Drop" policy when it comes to domestic battery cases. This means the State will still move forward with a domestic battery prosecution, even if the alleged victim recants their statements or wishes to drop the charges. Additionally, most counties have devoted extra resources to the formation of specialized prosecuting units that exclusively handle domestic battery cases. These extra resources go toward providing prosecutors with specialized training for domestic battery cases, hiring victim coordinators to ensure that alleged victims are cooperative with the prosecution of the case, and hiring investigators to locate and serve alleged victims with subpoenas to ensure their attendance at court proceedings.

Anyone accused of domestic battery faces an uphill battle. With the extra resources the State has at its disposal to prosecute domestic battery cases and the Legislature's willingness to create laws that stack the deck in the prosecution's favor, persons accused of domestic battery are essentially stepping into the box with 2 strikes against them. On top of everything else, there is a general public condemnation for domestic violence and it is often very difficult for perspective jurors to look past the allegations and be impartial when considering the evidence.

Anyone who has been accused of domestic battery, needs to consult with an attorney that regularly handles domestic battery cases within the county they are charged. Bringing in an out of town lawyer to handle a domestic battery case is often a mistake because every county and every courtroom within a county operates differently. You will want to speak with an attorney that is familiar with the prosecution practices for the State's Attorney's Office in that jurisdiction and the common practices for the judge within the domestic battery courtroom.

Can the alleged victim drop the charges?

As an Illinois Criminal Defense Attorney, I have consulted with hundreds of individuals who are facing domestic battery charges. The question that is asked most often is whether the alleged victim in the case can simply drop the charges. The short answer is no. In Illinois, domestic battery charges are prosecuted by the State's Attorney's Office and not the alleged victim. This means the prosecution of the case will continue despite the wishes of the alleged victim.

Many times, persons accused of domestic battery are eager to have the alleged victim contact the State's Attorney's Office to recant their statements or to ask the charge to be dismissed. This is often a mistake and can pose several dangers to the defense. If the State feels a defendant is trying to coerce a witness, they may file additional charges for witness tampering. For this reason, criminal defendants should always be strictly cautioned against communicating with potential witnesses for the State. Under Illinois law:

> A person who, with intent to deter any party or witness from testifying freely, fully and truthfully to any matter pending in any court, forcibly detains such party or witness, or communicates, directly or indirectly, to such party or witness any knowingly false information or a threat of injury or damage to the property or person of any individual or offers or delivers or threatens to withhold money or another

thing of value to any individual commits a
Class 3 felony.

Moreover, if the State suspects that the defendant coerced the alleged victim into not testifying against them, the prosecution may be able to admit the alleged victim's previous statements into evidence, even if they are not available to testify at trial. This is done under the theory of forfeiture by wrongdoing. Basically, if the court rules the defendant had a hand in making the alleged victim unavailable for trial, not only does the alleged victim's statements come into evidence but the defense forfeits their right to cross examination. Having the alleged victim's statements admitted into evidence without the ability to cross-examine can severely hinder the defense's case at trial.

Additionally, defendants in domestic battery cases are usually prohibited from contact with the alleged victim through bond conditions assigned by the court. This includes, speaking with the alleged victim, phone calls, text messages, social media, and sending messages through third parties. Should the Defendant violate these bond conditions they would be subject to a revocation of their bond, which would require them to stay in custody pending the resolution of their case, and possible new criminal charges for a violation of bond conditions.

Can the alleged victim simply change their story?

If an alleged victim decides to change their story prior to trial, this will not prevent the State from prosecuting the case. Should the alleged victim take the stand and give testimony that is significantly different than what they reported to the police, the State may attempt to impeach the alleged victim based on their prior statements, statements of third party witnesses, physical evidence such as photographs of injuries or ripped clothing, 911 calls, etc. This may seem unusual that the prosecution would be impeaching their own witness, but it is common practice in domestic battery cases.

Moreover, if a Defendant is caught trying to persuade a witness to testify in a manner that supports the Defendant's theory of the case, they could be charged with suborning perjury, a class 4 felony. Telling an alleged victim to make a statement that "nothing happened" will be interpreted by prosecutors and judges as criminal behavior and will likely result in new felony charges against the Defendant. Additionally, if the Defendant is caught trying to coerce a witness, it will have a severely negative impact on the pending domestic battery case and the prosecutor will be less likely to offer a favorable disposition prior to trial. Even if the witness does change their story, their original statements will still be admissible at trial. This is especially a concern for defendants who are in custody trying to contact alleged victims using the jail's phone systems, as all these calls are recorded and monitored by the jail staff.

When a person is charged with domestic battery and is held in custody, all their communications, except communications with their legal counsel, are subject to monitoring. This includes jail phone calls and in person visits. If the inmate attempts to contact the alleged victim in their case, the jail will send a copy of that communication to the State's Attorney's Office. Once the State's Attorney's Office receives the communication, they will determine whether to file additional charges.

Currently, more and more technology is being made available to inmates, such as laptops and ipads. This expands the means with which an inmate may attempt to make contact with the outside world. Even though these programs are fairly new, there have been several instances where an inmate has tried to use these technologies to contact witnesses in their case in an attempt to persuade them to change their story. All of these avenues of communication with the outside world are being monitored by the jail staff. If an inmate attempts to use an ipad, a laptop, or even another inmate to communicate with the alleged victim in their case, they will likely have additional charges filed against them.

Often times, alleged victims are weary of making any statements that are inconsistent with the original statement they made to the police. This is because most State's Attorneys Offices employ victim witness coordinators to assist in the prosecution of domestic battery cases. The primary job for a victim witness coordinator is to ensure that the victim will be available to testify and do so in a manner that is favorable to the prosecution. Most of the time, alleged victims are reminded about the penalties for filing a false police report and for perjuring themselves on the stand. These reminders serve to ensure an alleged victim's attendance at trial and that their testimony will be consistent with their previous statements to law enforcement.

Because of this, the alleged victim is often fearful of the possibility of criminal prosecution if they change their story. Victim witness coordinators also work closely with social service agencies like DCFS and may even threaten alleged victims with the prospect of losing custody of their children if they do not assist the state with the prosecution of the suspected abuser.

Spousal Privilege – Can my spouse be forced to testify against me?

Spousal privilege prevents one spouse from testifying against the other about *"communications which are intended to be confidential."* In order to assert spousal privilege about a marital communication, two elements must be satisfied:

(1) The communication must be an utterance or other expression intended to convey a message, and

(2) the message must be intended by the communicating spouse to be confidential *"in that it was conveyed in reliance on the confidence of the marital relationship."*

Courts have found that the privilege covers only those private exchanges which *"would not have been made but for the absolute confidence in, and induced by, the marital relationship"* and *"prompted by the affection, confidence, and loyalty engendered by such relationship."*

Spousal privilege is codified in 725 ILCS 5/115-16 and states as follows:

> In criminal cases, husband and wife may testify for or against each other. Neither, however, may testify as to any communication or admission made by either of them to the other or as to any conversation between them during marriage, except in cases in which either is charged with an offense against the person or property of the other...

Essentially, spousal privilege does not prevent a spouse from testifying about an alleged incident of domestic battery. First, the privilege only covers communications between spouses and does not apply to actions. Second, even if spousal privilege did cover actions, the spousal privilege can be waived by the alleged victim if they so choose. Finally, the Illinois statute that covers spousal privilege makes an exception for cases where one spouse is charged with an offense against the other.

The Confrontation Clause - What If The Alleged Victim Does Not Show Up For Trial?

The Confrontation Clause of the Sixth Amendment to the United States Constitution provides that "*...in all criminal prosecutions, the accused shall enjoy the right...to be confronted with the witnesses against him.*" However, the Illinois legislature has made special rules for domestic battery cases that may allow for the inclusion of statements from the alleged victim without them being present to testify at trial or being subject to cross-examination. This is codified in 725 ILCS 5/115-10.2

```
(a) In a domestic violence prosecution, a
statement, made by a [victim] that is not
specifically covered by any other hearsay
exception but having equivalent circumstantial
guarantees of trustworthiness, is not excluded
by the hearsay rule if the declarant is
identified as unavailable as defined in
subsection (c) and if the court determines
that:

  (1) the statement is offered as evidence of a
      material fact; and
  (2) the statement is more probative on the
      point for which it is offered than any
      other evidence which the proponent can
      procure through reasonable efforts; and
  (3) the general purposes of this Section and
      the interests of justice will best be
```

> served by admission of the statement into evidence.
>
> (b) A statement may not be admitted under this exception unless the proponent of it makes known to the adverse party sufficiently in advance of the trial or hearing to provide the adverse party with a fair opportunity to prepare to meet it, the proponent's intention to offer the statement, and the particulars of the statement, including the name and address of the declarant.

When alleged victims do not testify at trial, the admission of their accusatory statements under this code section, or through other hearsay exceptions, seems to run afoul of the confrontation clause, but courts have upheld the legislation as constitutional. As long as the State meets the 3 prongs for admission of the statements and provides the statements to the defense in advance of trial, they will be admitted into evidence, despite the unavailability of the alleged victim at trial.

Additionally, if the State has reason to believe that the defendant had a hand in making the alleged victim unavailable for trial they may attempt to admit inculpatory statements made by the alleged victim through the doctrine of forfeiture by wrongdoing. This is codified in Illinois statutes and has been upheld by the courts. However, prior to admitting the statements of the alleged victim, the State will need to show that the defendant intended to keep the alleged victim from testifying.

Witness Credibility

Many domestic battery charges arise out of situations where the alleged victim had other motivations for getting the defendant in trouble. For example, one party may be trying to gain an advantage over the other in a divorce or child custody case. There are other situations where a couple will have an argument and one party will lash out at the other and make exaggerated or false statements to the police while they are still upset about the argument. This will likely result in the other party being arrested and charged with domestic battery. Usually the party making the exaggerated statement will try to recant once the situation has cooled off. However, most prosecuting entities will continue to pursue charges despite the recanted statement. In either of these situations, the case will likely be set for trial and part of the defense strategy will be to attack the credibility of the complaining witness.

In the case where a witness has exaggerated their story and has since changed their version of what happened, it is often helpful to get that witness to put their new story into an affidavit. When getting an affidavit, it is important to be cautious of any no contact provisions that may be in place as a condition of bond. The defendant will usually be barred from attempting to contact a complaining witness directly, or even using someone else to contact them on their behalf in order to obtain an affidavit. It is usually best to allow the defense team to handle any contact with any witnesses in the case to avoid the potential for additional charges. Defense lawyers are allowed to interview any and all witnesses that the State may call at trial. However, the witnesses are not obligated to speak with any member of the defense team. Additionally, there is no right to a deposition of any witness in a criminal prosecution. This can make it difficult to know exactly what a witness will say on the stand if they are not willing to speak with the defense team prior to trial.

If the witness is willing to talk with the defense team and willing to write an affidavit clarifying the events that led to criminal charges, this can be helpful during negotiations and trial. While presenting the prosecutor with a recanting affidavit will rarely lead to a dismissal of pending charges, it is possible that the prosecutor will be more willing to amend or reduce the charge in the face of a recanting statement. If the prosecution refuses to negotiate, the affidavit may be used at trial to impeach the complaining witness, should they change their story back to a version more consistent with the State's theory of the case. If the witness testifies in a manner consistent with the affidavit given to the defense, then it is likely that the State will use the witness's original statement to law enforcement to impeach the witness in hopes of gaining a conviction. While a recanting affidavit can help in resolving a domestic battery case in a favorable manner, it rarely results in an outright dismissal and does not guarantee a win at trial.

If the complaining witness does not give a recanting statement and they are fabricating allegations to gain an advantage in a family case, then their credibility will have to be attacked by other means. A skilled defense attorney will look for any inconsistencies with the witness's version of events given to police and the one they are testifying to under oath during trial. If a witness's story keeps changing and is inconsistent with other witnesses version of events, then this will severely hinder that witness's credibility in front of a jury. Additionally, during a domestic battery investigation, police officers are trained to look for and photograph any injuries that are visible on the alleged victim. When a witness is fabricating a story to get the defendant arrested, the physical evidence will not line up with the witness's version of events. Often times, the witness will then try to cure their story on the stand, so it is consistent with the physical evidence. If a witness does this, they will be subject to impeachment with the previous statements they made to law enforcement.

In addition to any statements made to the police, a lot of law enforcement agencies are starting to employ body cameras. This allows the police to not only capture the statements made by a complaining witness, but to also see whether any injuries or marks of physical abuse are present at the time the complaint is made. When a witness is fabricating a story, the body camera footage can be a useful tool in impeaching that witness's credibility in front of a jury.

Medical Evidence

For a medical diagnosis to be admitted into evidence at trial, there needs to be expert testimony by a qualified medical professional. In the context of a domestic battery case, this professional is usually the emergency room doctor or physician that treated the alleged victim around the time of the alleged incident. Before the court will allow a medical doctor, or any other expert to give their opinion or conclusion concerning injuries or any specific diagnosis, a proper foundation must be laid to show that the expert is actually qualified to make such an opinion. This foundation usually consists of the purported expert explaining his education, background, work experience, and any publications they may have. After hearing this foundational testimony, the court will decide whether it will allow the witness to give their opinion on specific matters for which they are qualified. Even though a witness is qualified as an expert, they may only give expert opinions about their particular field of expertise. For example, it would be improper for an orthopedic surgeon to opine on whether a person had a psychological condition, because that is outside their field of practice.

If the prosecution wishes to have an expert witness testify at trial, they must make available to the defense team all information concerning the expert's qualifications. In addition to the expert's qualifications, the State must also turn over any reports created by the expert concerning the case, any evidence that was used in creating the reports, and any opinions that the expert will testify to at trial. This gives the defense team an opportunity to vet the expert's qualifications, challenge their conclusions, and find their own experts that may contradict the findings of the state's expert witness.

If the prosecution elects not to have an expert witness testify, they may still try to introduce medical conclusions through the testimony of lay persons, such as the alleged victim or third-party witnesses. This type of testimony is improper, and the defense team should object to it immediately and get an instruction from the court directing the jury to disregard any unqualified statement.

Motions in Limine – Setting the Ground Rules for Trial

Motions in limine (pronounced limb-in-ay) are motions that the court will rule on before trial outside the presence of the jury. These motions basically set the ground rules for what evidence and arguments may be presented at trial by each side. These motions are usually filed and addressed in advance of the trial. Both the Defense and State are allowed to file motions in limine and the judge will hear arguments and rule on each motion prior to the commencement of a jury trial.

The State will usually file a motion in limine to admit any hearsay evidence that maybe subject to a hearsay exception such as an excited utterance. Whenever a person testifies in court to what another person said, this is hearsay and is inadmissible unless it falls within one of the enumerated exceptions to the hearsay rule. One of the main exceptions under the Illinois Rules of Evidence is the excited utterance exception. According to Illinois Rule 803(b) an excited utterance is *"a statement relating to a startling event or condition made while the declarant was under the stress of excitement caused by the event or condition."*

Most of the time, the State will try to admit audio recordings of 911 calls and witness statements given to the police within close proximity to the alleged incident. In order to do this the State will have to file a motion in limine and present foundational evidence that the person making the statements was still affected by the event that they witnessed. If the court finds the state has met its burden and established the foundation for the excited utterance hearsay exception, the motion will be granted and the State may present the recordings/statements to the jury.

Likewise, the defense team will want to file their own motions in limine to try and exclude certain evidence and testimony that it believes the State will try to present. If the defense feels that some witness statements do not qualify for a hearsay exception, then it is usually best to pre-emptively file a motion in limine to bar the inclusion of any hearsay statements. This prevents the State from "accidentally" eliciting hearsay testimony from their witnesses. If the Jury hears inadmissible testimony, the judge will issue a statement telling the jury to disregard the testimony.

However, it is always best to prevent inadmissible evidence from being presented by the state, because who knows if the jury will actually follow the judge's instructions and disregard what they just heard.

Moreover, If the defense team suspects that the State will try to introduce a medical diagnosis without a qualified expert, then they should file a motion in limine to prevent such evidence. This is a standard practice that I have adopted anytime the state alleges an injury. Police officers, third party witnesses, and the alleged victim may only testify to what they saw. They may not talk about any medical conclusions, such as "I think the victim suffered a concussion." These witnesses, however, will be allowed to testify to any marks or bruises that they observed, but the defense must be on their toes when the State is eliciting this testimony, so the witness does not go beyond the scope of their qualifications. On one occasion during trial, a prosecutor showed the alleged victim pictures of bruises that were taken several days after an alleged incident and asked the question, "Do these pictures show the progression of the bruises from the night in question?" I immediately objected arguing the witness is not qualified to talk about how bruises progress over time, and the objection was sustained by the court. The witness was allowed to say those bruises were on her body several days after the incident but was not allowed to opine that those bruises progressed to their current state in the picture dating back to the alleged incident.

Self-Defense – What if I Was Attacked?

If you were attacked and forced to defend yourself, then its possible that self-defense may apply. Self-defense is an affirmative defense that will excuse the criminal conduct. Essentially an affirmative defense is like saying, "I did it, but I had a good reason to do it." In order to prove self-defense, the defendant needs to show that they were under an immediate threat of harm and committing the battery was the only way to extricate themselves from that potentially harmful situation.

In order to claim self-defense, the defense will need to file a notice of affirmative defense with the court in order to put the prosecution on notice that this defense will be used at trial. Once self-defense is filed, the defendant should also file a motion for disclosure to the defense asking the prosecution to turn over any violent criminal history for the alleged victim that the state is aware of. Courts have ruled when a defendant claims self-defense, any prior incidents of violent behavior committed by the alleged victim can potentially be admissible at trial. This includes convictions for any violent crimes and any incidents of violent behavior, even if they were not charged or reported to the police.

If the defense wishes to admit evidence of any prior incidents that show the alleged victim has a propensity for violence, they will have to file a motion-in-limine outlining exactly what they are seeking to admit at trial. The judge will hear the motion prior to trial and decide on whether the jury will be allowed to hear the evidence.

To admit previous convictions of violence by the alleged victim, the defense will need to obtain a certified copy of the conviction from the circuit clerk's office where the conviction occurred. There is usually a fee for certified documents, which varies by county, but is typically in the range of $10-$20. This document should be attached to the motion-in-limine and presented to the court in advance of the hearing.

To admit prior violent behavior of the alleged victim that was not charged, the defense will need to call a witness to testify about the violent incident. Details about the witness and what they will testify to should be contained in the motion-in-limine and presented to the court. The motion should be specific about what information the defense is seeking to present to the jury. The scope of behavior that may be admitted is very broad and the court will have a lot of discretion on what it considers violent in nature. One example of behavior that could possibly be admitted would be, if the alleged victim got in an argument while at a bar and shoved another person. Even though the police were not involved during this incident, the defense may still present it as evidence if they locate the person who was shoved at the bar and convince them to testify on their behalf.

Can My Prior History Be Used Against Me at Trial?

For the majority of criminal charges, a defendant's past criminal history will be excluded. There are a few exceptions to this rule, but for the most part, the State will be barred from presenting past criminal behavior as evidence of the defendant's propensity to commit crimes. For instance, in a DUI prosecution, the State will not be allowed to admit into evidence any prior DUI convictions the defendant may have. However, the Illinois legislature has made special rules for domestic battery prosecutions that allow the State to admit any prior incidents of domestic violence. These include convictions for domestic battery, incidents of domestic battery that were charged and did not lead to a conviction, and even incidents that were not charged nor reported to the police. This provision is codified in 725 ILCS 5/115-7.4 and has been upheld by the courts as not violating the defendant's constitutional rights.

> Evidence in domestic violence cases.
>
> (a) In a criminal prosecution in which the defendant is accused of an offense of domestic violence ... evidence of the defendant's commission of another offense or offenses of domestic violence is admissible, and may be considered for its bearing on any matter to which it is relevant.
>
> (b) In weighing the probative value of the evidence against undue prejudice to the defendant, the court may consider:
>
> > (1) the proximity in time to the charged or predicate offense;
> > (2) the degree of factual similarity to the charged or predicate offense; or
> > (3) other relevant facts and circumstances.
>
> (c) In a criminal case in which the prosecution intends to offer evidence under this Section, it must disclose the evidence, including statements of witnesses or a summary of the substance of any testimony, at a reasonable time in advance of trial, or during trial if the court excuses pretrial notice on good cause shown.
>
> (d) In a criminal case in which evidence is offered under this Section, proof may be made by specific instances of conduct, testimony as to reputation, or testimony in the form of an expert opinion, except that the prosecution may offer reputation testimony only after the opposing party has offered that testimony.

In order for the prosecution to admit this type of evidence, they must give the defense notice, specifying which witnesses and statements they plan to introduce. The statute requires this be done in advance of trial, unless they have a good reason, then they may be allowed to surprise the defense during the trial.

As soon as the defense receives notice that the prosecution plans to introduce this type of evidence, they should immediately file a motion to try and exclude the evidence based on relevancy, hearsay without an exception, and that its probative value is substantially outweighed by the risk of undue prejudice to the defendant. Additionally, the defense should argue that the previous event is too far attenuated from the present allegation to be relevant and that the facts of the previous incidents are distinguishable from the pending alleged charges, since these are statutory reasons to exclude the evidence.

What If The Police Never Read Me My Rights, Will My Case Be Dismissed?

This is a question that I have been asked numerous times. This myth seems to have been propagated through Hollywood TV shows and movies that portray a grizzly detective that makes a bust, then the criminal goes free on a technicality because they were never read their rights. This is not an accurate portrayal of our legal system and nowhere in the constitution of the United States or the State of Illinois are the police required to read a suspect their rights before, during, or after they are arrested.

So, what are Miranda Rights and why are they important? During the prosecution of any criminal case, the state may use any statement, previously made by the defendant, as evidence in trial. Even though these statements are technically hearsay, they fall into an exception to the hearsay rule because the defendant is a party opponent. Therefore, any statement the defendant makes to anyone, even a friend or family member, may be used as evidence to prosecute the case.

The only time inculpatory statements made by the defendant may possibly be excluded from evidence, is if the police interrogate the defendant in custody without first advising the defendant of his or her Miranda rights. This is not a simple thing to prove and there are a lot of variables in the equation. There is a mountain of case law, both federal and state, that the courts will consider in making a decision on the matter.

If the defendant believes that some inculpatory statements are subject to suppression, then the defense team should file a motion to suppress statements. Unlike most pre-trial motions, where the burden of proof will be on the moving party to prove their case, a motion to suppress statements is different, in that it will place the burden on the State to prove that the inculpatory statements were not obtained improperly.

Contained in the motion to suppress statements, the defendant should include sufficient allegations to create a prima facia case that would warrant the suppression of statements. Said another way, if all the allegations presented in the motion were proven to be true, then the law would require the suppression of the statements identified in the motion. Every motion to suppress statements should contain allegations listed below:

- The defendant was placed under arrest or in the custody of the police.
- The police questioned the defendant while in custody.

- During the in-custody interrogation, the defendant made the following statements
    - Statement 1
    - Statement 2
    - Statement 3
- That prior to the defendant making these statements, while in-custody, no one advised the defendant of his constitutional rights.

If the pleadings within the motion to suppress statements are incomplete, or do not create a prima facia case for suppression, the prosecutor will likely file a motion to strike. A motion to strike is filed by the non-moving party when they feel the moving party has not included sufficient allegations within their motion to establish a case that would warrant relief from the court. Essentially, a motion to strike says, even if everything you are claiming is true, the law says the statements would not be suppressed. Should a motion to strike get granted, the defendant will likely be given an opportunity to cure the pleadings and refile an amended motion to suppress statements.

As previously stated, there is a mountain of case law that the courts will consider when deciding these motions. If at all possible, the defense should include cites to relevant cases with similar fact patterns when filing a motion to suppress statements. This will give the court an opportunity to review the favorable case law prior to hearing the evidence on the motion.

When ruling on a motion to suppress statements, one of the biggest hurdles is proving that the defendant was actually in-custody at the time the police were conducting their questioning. There is no bright line rule for when a person is in-custody. The courts will look at several factors in making that determination, including: How did the person get to the place of the interrogation? How many police officers were present? Were the officers armed? Was the defendant separated from his or her family? Was the defendant in handcuffs? Would an objectively reasonable person feel they were free to walk away and not answer the officers questions (in fairness, no objectively reasonable person feels free to walk away from the police, but courts regularly indicate otherwise in their rulings).

Usually when a person is put in handcuffs and placed in the back of a police car, they are under arrest and "in-custody" for purposes of Miranda. However, the courts will consider all the circumstances involved and have found instances where a person was restrained and in the back of a police car but not "in-custody" for purposes of Miranda. Also, courts have found situations where a person was not in handcuffs but did consider them "in-custody" for purposes of Miranda. Each case is unique and usually requires extensive legal analysis, case law research, and creative arguments on behalf of the defense team.

Should the defense prevail on a motion to suppress statements, the case is not over. The State will still move forward with prosecuting the case. However, they will not be allowed to use any inculpatory statements that were obtained improperly. In a lot of cases, the most damning evidence against a defendant are the statements made to police. Excluding these statements can have a significant impact on the case, the negotiation process, and the odds of getting a not-guilty verdict at trial.

CHAPTER 7

POSSIBLE COMPANION CHARGES

If a person is charged with domestic battery, there may be other companion charges that accompany the offense. These companion charges usually stem from the same incident that led to the domestic battery arrest and may serve to substantially increase the prospective jail time and/or fines. These charges will be prosecuted at the same time with the domestic battery charge.

Criminal Damage to Property

This is a common companion charge because the majority of domestic battery allegations involve arguments where items in the living space are broken during an altercation. If a witness or an alleged victim is trying to call the police and their phone is broken or damaged during the incident, then the defendant will likely be charged criminal damage to property.

Criminal damage to property is defined by 720 ILCS 5/21-1 and applies to anyone who knowingly damages the property of another. It is ok if you break your own stuff, but you cannot break anyone else's stuff. For couples who are married, the property will be considered co-owned by both parties and any damage to marital property could result in a criminal damage to property charge.

Criminal damage to property is usually charged as a class A misdemeanor, punishable by up to 1 year in jail and a fine of up to $2,500. If the alleged damage exceeds $500, then the charge may be enhanced to a class 4 felony, punishable by up to 3 years in prison. With the cost of the average iPhone being well north of $500, felony criminal damage to property charges are becoming more prevalent, especially when associated with domestic battery cases.

Interfering with the Reporting of Domestic Violence

This charge is a class A misdemeanor, punishable by up to 1 year in jail and fines and costs of up to $2,500. It is defined in 720 ILCS 5/12-3.5 as *"a person ... after having committed an act of domestic violence, he or she knowingly prevents or attempts to prevent the victim of or a witness ... from calling a 9-1-1 emergency telephone system, obtaining medical assistance, or making a report to any law enforcement official."*

The usual circumstance where this offense is charged is when the alleged victim claims they were trying to call police and the defendant took the phone out of their hands. According to the statute, that alleged behavior would be enough for a conviction.

Unlawful Restraint

Unlawful restraint is a class 4 felony, punishable by up to 3 years in prison. This is a serious charge and is intended to punish offenders who are holding victims captive against their will. However, I have seen overzealous prosecutors charge unlawful restraint when a defendant is simply standing in front of a door during an argument. A lot of times, prosecutors will add a charge for unlawful restraint in the hopes of getting a defendant to plea to the lesser domestic battery charge.

Unlawful restraint is defined by 720 ILCS 5/10-3. *"A person commits the offense of unlawful restraint when he or she knowingly without legal authority detains another."* Because the language is vague, there is a wide range of behaviors that may be encompassed by the statute. The vagueness of the statute is why prosecutors like charging unlawful restraint, in the hopes of encouraging a plea to a lesser charge.

Violation of an Order of Protection

Orders of Protection are civil in nature and are often accompanied with domestic battery charges. To get an order of protection, a person needs to file a petition with the court and have a hearing in front of a judge. Once the civil order of protection is granted, the Respondent will be prevented from doing any of the activities listed in the order. The most common thing will be for the Respondent to stay away from the Petitioner and not have any contact with them, either directly or indirectly. Even though an order of protection is civil, should the Respondent violate the conditions of the order, they would then be charged criminally.

Proving an order of protection has been violated is usually not a difficult task for a prosecutor. The most common way an order of protection is violated is by sending a text message or contact through social media. Since most orders of protection prohibit any form of contact between Petitioner and Respondent, sending any type of message would violate the order. This is applicable, even if the Petitioner initiates contact. Orders of protection are one way and do not restrict the activities of the Petitioner. Therefore, it is lawful for the Petitioner to text a Respondent, but as soon as the Respondent sends a reply text message to the Petitioner, the Respondent will be in violation of the order of protection.

Violation of an order of protection is a class A misdemeanor for a first offense, punishable by up to one year in jail and a fine of up to $2,500. Any subsequent offense for a violation of an order of protection can be charged as a class 4 felony punishable by up to 3 years in prison.

Criminal Trespass to Residence

Criminal trespass to residence is defined by 720 ILCS 5/19-4 and states *"A person commits criminal trespass to a residence when, without authority, he or she knowingly enters or remains within any residence, including a house trailer that is the dwelling place of another."* This is a class A misdemeanor punishable by up to 1 year in jail and a fine of up to $2,500. If there are allegations of another person being present, which is usually the case when associated with a domestic battery case, then the charge can be enhanced to a class 4 felony punishable by up to 3 years in prison.

This charge usually comes about when the alleged victim and the defendant are not living together. Most of the time, this charge accompanies a domestic battery that takes place at the alleged victim's dwelling.

Home Invasion

Home Invasion a class X felony and is not eligible for probation. It is defined in 720 ILCS 5/19-6(a)(2). *"A person ... commits home invasion when without authority he or she knowingly enters the dwelling place of another when he or she knows or has reason to know that one or more persons is present ... and ... Intentionally causes any injury...to any person within the dwelling place."*

The minimum sentence for a home invasion is 6 years in the department of corrections. While it is rare for this charge to be associated with a domestic battery incident, it does happen. Usually, these are cases that should be charged as a misdemeanor domestic battery and possibly a criminal trespass to residence. However, if an overzealous assistant state's attorney is making the charging decision, they may end up filing charges for home invasion. This all goes back to prosecutorial discretion. The legislature assumes that prosecutors will look at all the circumstances surrounding an incident and charge it accordingly. However, there are some prosecutors out there that just want to charge the biggest felony possible in all cases.

CHAPTER 8

POSSIBLE WAYS TO RESOLVE A DOMESTIC BATTERY CASE

How you choose to resolve your domestic battery case can have a significant impact on your life. In addition to any criminal penalties, such as jail time and fines, there may also be collateral consequences not explicitly listed in the disposition order. If you are convicted of domestic battery in Illinois, even on your first offense, you will have a permanent criminal conviction on your record that can never be sealed or expunged, and you will never be allowed to legally possess a firearm. This can affect your job, educational opportunities and even where you live. There are only a limited number of ways that a domestic battery case can be resolved.

Plea Bargain

The most common way a domestic battery case is resolved is by reaching an agreement with the State's Attorney's Office. A plea bargain may include a disposition to the original charge, an amended charge, or a reduced charge. Pleading to an amended charge is preferential, because domestic battery cases are not eligible for any special dispositions, like court supervision, that will lead to a dismissal of the charges upon successful completion of the sentence. It is possible that the prosecutor, when presented with appropriate mitigation and after consultation with the alleged victim, may be willing to amend the charge to battery or reckless conduct, which are eligible for court supervision. Should you receive court supervision on a reckless conduct or a battery charge, even if the charge was amended from domestic battery, then your case will be dismissed pending successful completion of the court supervision sentence. After your supervision is complete, you may be able to get the offense completely expunged from your record.

Open Plea

If the prosecutor is not willing to offer acceptable terms in exchange for a plea of guilty, then you may have the judge determine the sentence. This is usually referred to as an open plea or a blind plea. Because there is no agreement in place, it will be left solely up to the judge to determine the sentence. The judge may return any sentence that is within the sentencing range for the charge that was pled to. For a misdemeanor domestic battery, this will involve a permanent criminal conviction, up to one year in the county jail, conditional discharge or probation up to 2 years, and additional terms and conditions that usually include participation in counselling and attending a victim impact panel.

It is possible for the prosecutor to dismiss companion charges or even amend the original charge in exchange for an open plea. Once the charge is agreed on, the defendant will sign a guilty plea in open court and the case will be set over for a sentencing hearing. During a sentencing hearing, the court will hear evidence and the judge will decide the appropriate sentence for the charge that was pled to.

The prosecutor may even be willing to offer a "cap" on their sentencing recommendation in exchange for a plea of guilty. At the end of a sentencing hearing, the judge will ask each side for their recommendation on what the sentence should be. Usually the defense will ask for the minimum sentence and the prosecution will ask for something more. By agreeing to a cap, the prosecutor will be bound to make a certain recommendation during the sentencing hearing. The judge, however, is not bound by any recommendations and it is possible for the judge to return a sentence that is greater than what the prosecution is recommending. This, however, is rare and the judge will usually pick a sentence that is in-between the recommendation of the two parties.

402 Conference

A 402 conference is a special conference that allows the judge to get involved in negotiations for the case. If the defense and the prosecutor are unable to reach an agreement, then it is possible to ask the judge what sentence he or she would likely give should the case go to a sentencing hearing. This conference is conducted in the judge's chambers and is attended by the Defense Attorney, the Prosecutor and the judge. Both the prosecution and the defense have to agree to this conference before it can take place. You are not legally entitled to have a 402 conference and if the prosecutor does not agree to it, then it will not take place.

If possible, it is always advisable to conduct a 402 conference prior to an open plea. The judge will recommend a sentence that may be better than what the state is offering. Neither party is bound by the judge's recommendation and if the defendant is dissatisfied with the recommendation, they may continue to negotiate the case with the prosecutor or set the case for trial. It has been my experience that if the judge makes a recommendation, the prosecutor will amend his offer, consistent with the recommendation, in order to resolve the case.

Dismissal

If the prosecution concedes that the evidence in the case is not sufficient to obtain a conviction, they may choose to dismiss the case. While possible, it is rare for a prosecutor to voluntarily dismiss a domestic battery case. Dismissals usually come in 2 forms when dealing with domestic battery cases. Either, the prosecution feels the evidence so overwhelmingly points to the defendant's innocence that they are ethically bound to dismiss the case, or the more likely scenario, the case is set for trial and the prosecution is not ready to proceed for one reason or another, then the prosecutor will voluntarily dismiss the case before jeopardy attaches. If the latter is the reason for the dismissal, the prosecution will have the option of refiling the charges, as long as they are within the statute of limitations.

Not Guilty Verdict

If your case is taken to trial and the prosecutor is unable to present sufficient evidence for the jury or a judge to find you guilty beyond a reasonable doubt, then a not guilty verdict will be entered. Once you are found not guilty, you will not be subject to any of the fines or penalties that are associated with the case and you will be eligible to have the case expunged from your record.

Guilty Verdict

If your case is taken to trial and the prosecutor convinces the jury or a judge that you are guilty beyond a reasonable doubt, then a judgment of conviction will enter against you. After the conviction is entered, the case will be set for a sentencing hearing where a judge will determine the sentence. Prior to a sentencing hearing, the judge will order a pre-sentence investigation of the defendant. This investigation will look into the defendant's prior criminal history, family situation, nature of the offense, effects on the victim and the victim's family, and anything else deemed relevant by the investigator. The investigator will also meet with the defendant and get information and statements that will be included in a report that summarizes the investigation. This report will be made available to all parties and the judge prior to a sentencing hearing.

Sentencing Hearing

After an open plea or a guilty verdict at trial, the case will be set for a sentencing hearing whereby a judge will determine the sentence. At a sentencing hearing, both the defense and the prosecution will be allowed to present evidence and make recommendations as to what the appropriate sentence should be. Usually the prosecution will present statements from the victim, the victim's family, and may even have the victim testify in court. Additionally, the prosecution will make a proffer about the facts of the case including any aggravating details, such as injuries sustained by the victim, if weapons were used, whether any children witnessed the incident, etc.

Likewise, the defense may present evidence that tends to mitigate the offense. Usually, the defense will submit affidavits of support from family, friends, and co-workers. Additionally, the defense may call witnesses that will testify to the defendant's good moral character. The defendant may also take the stand but this is not recommended because they would be subject to cross-examination by the prosecutor.

Instead of taking the stand, it is recommended that the defendant prepare a statement in allocution. A statement in allocation is a statement that is made by the defendant, in open court, after all evidence has been presented but prior to closing arguments by the lawyers. During this statement, the defendant will be given an opportunity to mitigate the charge by accepting responsibility, humanize themselves, and presenting any special circumstance that may have led to the criminal behavior. The reason a statement in allocution is preferred over taking the stand is because these statements are not subject to cross examination by the prosecution. It is recommended that the defendant put a lot of time and effort into creating their statement in allocution and have it reviewed by defense counsel prior to presenting it in court. Always have this statement printed out so it can be available should you get stuck. The courtroom is a stressful place, especially for a person who has so much on the line and is probably speaking in court for the first time. Addressing the judge with a gallery full of people, which may include the victim and their family, can be an unnerving task. I've seen lots of people freeze up under the stress of talking in court. If you must make a statement in allocution, you should print it out, practice it, and have a family member listen to it. The judge will place a lot of weight on this statement, so its best to be over-prepared.

Once the evidence is presented to the court, the judge will determine the sentence. The judge is only allowed to consider the statutory factors in aggravation and mitigation. The statutory factors in mitigation are listed in 730 ILCS 5/5-5-3.1 and all factors that apply should be argued by the defense.

```
(1) The defendant's criminal conduct neither
    caused nor threatened serious physical harm to
    another.

(2) The defendant did not contemplate that his
    criminal conduct would cause or threaten
    serious physical harm to another.

(3) The defendant acted under a strong
    provocation.

(4) There were substantial grounds tending to
    excuse or justify the defendant's criminal
    conduct, though failing to establish a
    defense.
```

(5) The defendant's criminal conduct was induced or facilitated by someone other than the defendant.

(6) The defendant has compensated or will compensate the victim of his criminal conduct for the damage or injury that he sustained.

(7) The defendant has no history of prior delinquency or criminal activity or has led a law-abiding life for a substantial period of time before the commission of the present crime.

(8) The defendant's criminal conduct was the result of circumstances unlikely to recur.

(9) The character and attitudes of the defendant indicate that he is unlikely to commit another crime.

(10) The defendant is particularly likely to comply with the terms of a period of probation.

(11) The imprisonment of the defendant would entail excessive hardship to his dependents.

(12) The imprisonment of the defendant would endanger his or her medical condition.

(13) The defendant was a person with an intellectual disability as defined in Section 5-1-13 of this Code.

(14) The defendant sought or obtained emergency medical assistance for an overdose and was convicted of a Class 3 felony or higher possession, manufacture, or delivery of a controlled, counterfeit, or look-alike substance or a controlled substance analog under the Illinois Controlled Substances Act or a Class 2 felony or higher possession, manufacture or delivery of methamphetamine under the Methamphetamine Control and Community Protection Act.

(15) At the time of the offense, the defendant is or had been the victim of domestic violence and the effects of the domestic violence

tended to excuse or justify the defendant's criminal conduct. As used in this paragraph (15), "domestic violence" means abuse as defined in Section 103 of the Illinois Domestic Violence Act of 1986.

(16) At the time of the offense, the defendant was suffering from a serious mental illness which, though insufficient to establish the defense of insanity, substantially affected his or her ability to understand the nature of his or her acts or to conform his or her conduct to the requirements of the law.

(17) At the time of the offense, the defendant was suffering from post-partum depression or post-partum psychosis which was either undiagnosed or untreated, or both, and this temporary mental illness tended to excuse or justify the defendant's criminal conduct and the defendant has been diagnosed as suffering from post-partum depression or post-partum psychosis, or both, by a qualified medical person and the diagnoses or testimony, or both, was not used at trial.

The Factors in Aggravation are listed in 730 ILCS 5/5-5-3.2 and, for the most part, are the inverse of the mitigation factors. The legislature also added several factors in aggravation that are offense specific for charges other than domestic battery. Because there are so many factors in aggravation, I will not list them here, but they can be found by doing an internet search on the statute number listed above.

GLOSSARY

402 conference – A 402 conference is governed by Illinois Supreme Court Rule 402. Essentially if the parties are unable to come to agreeable terms to resolve a pending case, they may ask the judge to get involved in negotiations. Both parties must agree to conduct a 402 conference before it may take place. Attendance in a 402 conference is limited to the Defense attorney, the prosecutor and the judge. The defendant and the alleged victim will not be allowed to attend. During the conference, the attorneys do not have to follow the rules of evidence and the judge may hear facts about the defendant and the alleged victim that are not admissible at a trial or a hearing. The judge will make a recommendation about what the sentence might be should the defendant open plea to the charges. Either party is free to reject the recommendation of the judge. Conducting a 402 conference does not obligate the defendant to plead guilty and the defendant may still have a trial.

Affirmative Defense - A defense in which the defendant introduces evidence, which, if found to be credible, will negate criminal liability even if it is proven that the defendant committed the alleged acts.

Bench Trial – A lawful proceeding in Illinois whereby a judge, not a jury, makes a determination as to the defendant's guilt or innocence. If a defendant wishes to take their case to trial, they must decide whether they want a trial by jury or trial by judge. The defendant is the only person that can decide what type of trial to have in their case. The judge, the prosecutor and even the defendant's attorney cannot force the defendant to choose one type of trial over the other. Prior to setting a bench trial, the defendant must make a knowing and voluntary waiver of trial by jury.

Blind Plea – See open plea

Bond Conditions – In addition to posting a specified amount of money to ensure the defendant's appearance in court, there may be other court-imposed requirements that the defendant must abide by to be released while the case is pending trial. Usual bond conditions for domestic battery cases include no contact with the alleged victim, the alleged victim's residence, be subject to drug and alcohol testing, and in some cases, attend anger management or partner abuse intervention treatment.

Conditional Discharge – A form of non-reporting probation that allows the probation department to monitor a defendant to ensure they are complying with all the terms of their court order, without the requirement that the defendant regularly meet with a probation officer.

Day-for-Day Credit – Most jail sentences in Illinois are served with day-for-day credit, or 50% of the imposed sentence. For instance, if a defendant is sentence to 90 days in jail, and the sentence is subject to day-for-day credit, then the defendant would only have to serve 45 days. There are certain circumstances where day-for-day credit will not apply. For sentences to the Department of Corrections, day-for-day credit does not apply to any charge subject to truth-in-sentencing, which would require the offender to serve 75%, 85%, or 100% of the sentence as defined by the statute. If an offender is sentenced to local jail time, day-for-day credit will not apply to charges that have a mandatory minimum sentence, or in cases where physical harm is inflicted on the victim.

Excited Utterance – An exception to the hearsay rule that allows the admission of an out of court statement, when the statement is made by a person in response to a startling or shocking event or condition. The statement must be spontaneously made by the declarant while still under the stress or excitement from the event or condition. The subject matter and content of the statement must relate to event or condition.

Expert Witness – A witness that is allowed to offer his or her opinion at trial about a particular aspect of the case for which they are uniquely qualified. Usually, courts prohibit witnesses from offering their opinions as testimony. However, if it can be shown that a witness has necessary qualifications and experience within their field, the court may view that witness as an expert and allow the witness to opine about matters that are within their field of expertise. Generally speaking, experts may testify about their conclusions in a case so long as their analysis is scientifically sound. In reaching their conclusions, experts may rely on the same sorts of evidence that people in their profession normally rely on in their work, even if the evidence is otherwise inadmissible in court. For example, a doctor may testify about his analysis of X-rays, even though the X-rays would normally be considered hearsay.

Expungement – A legal process whereby the court orders the arrest and case information to be erased from the state records, as if it had never happened. Currently there are no mechanisms in Illinois to have a domestic battery conviction expunged.

Grand Jury – A hearing where a prosecutor from the State's Attorney Office will present evidence to a panel of 12 members of the community in order to determine if probable cause exists to charge an individual with a felony offense. The Constitution and laws of Illinois provide that no person shall be brought to trial for a crime punishable by imprisonment in the penitentiary unless either the initial charge has been brought by indictment of a grand jury or the person has been given a prompt preliminary hearing and a judge has found probable cause. The grand jury is presented with evidence and is asked if probable cause exists for the state to proceed with felony charges. Should the grand jury find probable cause, then a bill of indictment is returned and tendered to the defendant. Unlike a jury for a criminal trial where the jury must be unanimous to convict a defendant, in an Illinois grand jury, only 9 jurors must agree for the State to proceed forward with felony charges against the defendant.

Hearsay - An out-of-court statement offered to prove the truth of matter asserted. Generally, hearsay evidence is not admissible at trial, but there are many exceptions to the hearsay rule. In the context of a domestic battery cases, the legislature has added additional exceptions to the hearsay rule that make it easier for the admission of hearsay statements from the alleged victim, even if they are not available to testify at trial.

I-bond – see Recognizance bond

Jury Trial – A lawful proceeding in Illinois in which 12 members of the community make a determination as to the defendant's guilt or innocence. These 12 members are selected from a pool of approximately 50 potential jurors. The prosecution, the defense, and the court will be allowed to ask the potential jurors question to ensure they can be fair and impartial in rendering a verdict. The verdict must be unanimous among all 12 jurors. If the jury cannot come to a unanimous decision after extended deliberation, commonly referred to as a hung jury, then the court will dismiss the jury without returning a verdict. If no verdict is returned, the charges will still pending against the defendant and the parties may renegotiate the case or reset the case for trial.

Miranda Rights – These are constitutional rights, such as the right to remain silent and the right to have an attorney present during police interrogations. Prior to conducting an in-custody interrogation of an individual, police are required to advise the individual of these rights. Should the officer not advise the individual of these rights, any statement made by the individual might be excluded from evidence.

Motion for Discovery – This is a motion, when filed by the defense, that will require the state to produce any and all information, including possibly exculpatory evidence, related to the prosecution of a particular offense.

Motion in Limine – This is a motion that is usually filed and ruled on prior to a jury trial. These motions may be filed by either the prosecution or defense and seek to limit the evidence and arguments the other side may present. The purpose of this motion is to prevent the interjection of irrelevant and inadmissible evidence that may be prejudicial.

Motion to Strike – A request that the judge eliminate all or part of the other party's pleading. This is usually in the context of one party filing a motion which does not make a prima facia case for which the court may grant relief.

Motion to Suppress Statements – This is a motion filed by the defense that alleges the state has collected statements from the defendant pursuant to an in-custody interrogation, prior to the defendant being mirandized. This motion would seek to exclude the improperly collected statements from evidence. Unlike other motions filed by the defense, where the moving party has the burden of proof, a motion to suppress statements will place the burden on the State to show that the statements were not collected improperly.

Open Plea – An open plea is sometimes referred to as a blind plea. This is when the defense and the prosecution are unable to reach a fully negotiated agreement and the defense is asking the judge to determine the appropriate sentence. After a defendant pleads guilty to the charge, the case will be set for a sentencing hearing where each side may call witnesses, present evidence, make arguments, and give the court recommendations about what they believe is an appropriate sentence. After hearing the evidence, the judge will determine the sentence. Sometimes open pleas can involve a partial agreement between the parties. For instance, the State may be willing to dismiss some of the companion charges or offer a cap on their recommendation to the judge should the defendant plead guilty. If a cap is part of the plea, its important to know that the judge is not bound by the recommendations of the cap and may go above the cap. While it is a rare situation for the judge to exceed the recommendations from the State, it does happened and it something that the defendant should be aware of prior to conducting an open plea with a cap.

Partner Abuse Intervention Program (PAIP) – This is a counselling program designed to help abusers learn how to stop abusing their partners. Pursuant to any domestic battery disposition, the defendant will usually be required to complete this program. This is a 6 month program and the participant will be required to attend class once per week. Should the participant miss more than 3 classes, he or she would be required to restart the program.

Plea bargain – During the pendency of a case, the defense and prosecution are free to negotiate terms to possibly resolve the case. These terms may involve an amended charge, a reduced charge, or a dismissal of companion charges. Should the parties come to an agreement, then they must present their agreement to the court for approval. If the court accepts the agreement, the case is resolved and the terms of the agreement become order of the court. If the court rejects the agreement, the court may give guidance to the parties about how the agreement may be modified so it is acceptable to the court.

Pre-Sentence Investigation (PSI) – An investigation into the history of a defendant convicted of a crime. This is conducted prior to a sentencing hearing and is used to determine if there are any aggravating or mitigating factors about the defendant. This investigation is usually conducted by the probation department and includes an interview with the defendant. At the conclusion of the pre-sentence investigation, a PSI report will be forwarded to the prosecution, the defendant, and the court. This report will contain the results of the investigation which will include any statements the defendant made, the factual basis of the offense, information about the defendant's family members, living situation, work history, any treatment previously completed, criminal history, and anything else the investigating officer deems relevant to the proceeding.

Pretrial Conference – A pretrial conference is a court hearing that precedes trial. During this court appearance, the court will be looking for guidance from the parties to determine the status of the pending case. The parties will indicate whether they believe the case will be resolved with a plea or litigated at trial.

Pretrial Services – This department is responsible for collecting and analyzing information about a defendant used in determining risk. This department will also make recommendations to the court when setting bond for a defendant concerning conditions of release and whether a cash bond should be posted. Pretrial services will also monitor defendants who are released on bond to ensure they are complying with all conditions of release including drug testing, participating in treatment, curfew requirements, etc.

Pre-Trial Services Report – This report is completed by the pretrial services department after a defendant is arrested for a domestic battery or felony offense and prior to the court setting bond. This report will contain information about the defendant's family, work history, criminal history, education, etc. The report will assess whether the defendant is a danger to the community or a flight risk and will make recommendations about what bond conditions should be placed on the defendant's release. The judge may consider this report when setting bond, but the judge is not bound by any of the recommendations.

Probation – In lieu of a sentence to the department of corrections, or an extended stay in the county jail, the court may sentence a defendant to a term of probation. While on probation, a defendant will have to follow certain rules and guidelines, including regularly reporting to a probation officer. The probation officer will monitor the defendant to ensure compliance with all terms of the court ordered requirements. Usual requirements involve, not using drugs or alcohol, attending counselling, and most importantly, not violating the law while on the probated sentence.

Recognizance bond – This is a bond that does not require the defendant to post any money to be released. Even though no cash is required, there may still be conditions on the defendant's release, such as random drug testing, or not having contact with the alleged victim.

Sealing – A court ordered process whereby the details about a particular criminal case are hidden from the public, but will still be available to the courts, the police, and certain employers that are required to do background checks, such as hospitals and schools.

Self Defense – An affirmative defense whereby the defendant is required to use force to protect himself from potential injury.

Sentence Cap – At a sentencing hearing, both the defense and prosecution will make recommendations to the judge on what they believe is an appropriate sentence for the pending charges to which the defendant has either pled guilty or been found guilty. In certain circumstances, the prosecution may offer a cap on their recommendation. This is usually done in consideration of the defendant pleading guilty. When offering a cap, the prosecution is bound by their recommendation, but the judge is not. While rare, it is possible for the judge to enter a sentence that is above the cap recommended by the prosecutor.

Sentencing Hearing – A hearing that takes place after a defendant is found guilty at trial, or the defendant pleads guilty prior to trial without having an agreement with the prosecution (blind plea). At this hearing, both the prosecution and the defense will be given an opportunity to present evidence to the judge and make sentence recommendations for what they believe is an appropriate disposition for the pending charge. The defendant will be afforded an opportunity to make a statement in allocution after all the evidence is presented. At the conclusion of the hearing, the judge will sentence the defendant based on the evidence, recommendation of the parties, prior criminal history of the defendant, information contained in the pre-sentence report, the facts of the case, and the defendant's statement in allocution.

Spousal Privilege – This is a privilege that prevents one spouse from testifying in court about statements another spouse made during the confidences of the marriage. The following must be satisfied for spousal privilege to apply: (1) the communication must be an utterance or other expression intended to convey a message, and (2) the message must be intended by the communicating spouse to be confidential "in that it was conveyed in reliance on the confidence of the marital relationship. Additionally, courts have found that the privilege covers only those private exchanges which "would not have been made but for the absolute confidence in, and induced by, the marital relationship," and "prompted by the affection, confidence, and loyalty engendered by such relationship."

Statement in allocution – A statement made by a defendant near the conclusion of a sentencing hearing. This is an opportunity for the defendant to address the court directly, without being subject to cross-examination. The defendant can inform the court about any special circumstances surrounding the offense and mention other factors in mitigation for the court to consider prior to passing sentence.

Truth in Sentencing – A requirement whereby offenders convicted of an enumerated list of violent crimes are required to serve 75%, 85% or 100% of their sentence. Most offenses in Illinois only require offenders to serve 50% of their sentence.

Victim Impact Panel (VIP) – A forum for crime victims to address a group of offenders about the impact that a crime has had on their lives. These panels usually involve three to six victims addressing the audience for about 15 minutes each telling their story in a nonjudgmental manner. Attendance in a victim impact panel is usually required pursuant to any disposition for domestic battery.

Voir Dire - The process by which prospective jurors are questioned about their backgrounds and potential biases before being chosen to sit on a jury. During this process, the prosecution, the defense, and the judge may question potential jurors. If during the questioning it is determined that a potential juror cannot be fair and impartial, then the judge may remove that juror for cause. If either the prosecution or defense believe a potential juror would be detrimental to their side, and that juror is not subject to removal for cause, then they may remove that juror by using a challenge. Each side has a predetermined number of challenges that varies based on the severity of the offense. Either side may use a challenge at any time during the voir dire process to remove a potential juror.

ABOUT THE AUTHOR

Illinois Criminal Defense Attorney Jonathan James has successfully represented hundreds of clients charged with domestic battery. He is a member of the Illinois State Bar Association and has received several awards including: The National Trial Lawyers "Top 40 Under 40", The National Academy of Criminal Defense Attorneys "Top 10 Under 40", and the Lawyers of Distinction "Top 10% in the USA" in the area of criminal defense.

Mr. James graduated with a Bachelor of Science degree from Clemson University where he received several awards including Dean's List, President's List and was a member of the Upsilon Pi Epsilon Honor Society. Mr. James attended Northern Illinois University College of Law where he graduated with a degree of Juris Doctor. Currently Mr. James runs The Law Office of Jonathan James, LLC, which has offices in Rockford, IL and Dekalb, IL.

For more information about his criminal defense practice, visit his website at IllinoisDomesticBattery.com. To schedule an appointment to speak with an experienced domestic battery defense attorney call our office at 779.500.0167

www.ingramcontent.com/pod-product-compliance
Lightning Source LLC
Chambersburg PA
CBHW030950240526
45463CB00016B/2246